Samuel S. Spaulding

Spaulding's History of Crown Point, N. Y.

From 1800-1874

Samuel S. Spaulding

Spaulding's History of Crown Point, N. Y.
From 1800-1874

ISBN/EAN: 9783337269104

Printed in Europe, USA, Canada, Australia, Japan

Cover: Foto ©ninafisch / pixelio.de

More available books at **www.hansebooks.com**

SPAULDING'S

HISTORY

OF

Crown Point, N. Y.

From 1800 to 1874.

TO
CHARLES F. HAMMOND, Esq.,

Who, for many years has been identified with the History and Progress of Crown Point, this little
work is respectfully dedicated

By the Author.

TO THE READER:

In writing the history of Old Crown Point, it carries
me back to the scenes of my childhood, and creates a
feeling of sadness mingled with pleasure; but as it has
been, either my good or bad fortune, to be an inhabitant
of this town from my infancy, my memory dates back
to near the beginning of this century; and it shall be my
sole object and aim, while writing this history, to show
to the reader Crown Point as it Was, at my earliest mo-
ments, and its rise and progress, from time to time, and
the cause thereof, hoping, if he has the patience to fol-
low me through these vicissitudes of human life for three
score years and ten, he never will be sorry for the pains
taken.

The Author.

CHAPTER I.

It is well authenticated in history that the lands in the most favorable localities along the shores of Lake Champlain, was cleared and settled by the French in the days of the French wars, and perhaps prior to that date ; and of course some of the lands on the immediate shores of the lake in Crown Point, were cleared and settled at the same time. But little was known of the interior of Crown Point, particularly the west part of the town, until about the year 1800, except reports from hunters and trappers, who roamed the forest in quest of wild game, of which the country then abounded. They reported there was a tract of beautiful settling land in Crown Point about ten miles square embracing Putnam's Creek and its tributaries within its limits, and that this tract of land was timbered with beautiful hard wood and well watered with never failing springs of the purest water ; together with the natural advantages of the country, made it a very inviting spot for young men of that day, of strong nerve and will, who felt disposed to grapple with the old primeval forest. They also reported that immediately west and joining this tract of land were the fine old hills and mountain peaks of the Adirondaks situated on the head-waters of the Hudson River, of which I will speak of more fully hereafter.

This news circulated through the country and reached

several of the New England States, and inspired a great many young men of that day with a strong desire to see and explore the 'promised land,' as it was then called in York State. At this time my father, Stephen Spaulding, resided in Salisbury, Vt. He among the rest caught the York fever, as it was then called, and started in company with several others in September, 1800, to explore these lands. Their intention was to ascend every hill and mountain within their reach until they found one that would overlook all the rest. After exploring the wilderness for two days, sleeping on the ground at night, the third day, late in the afternoon, found them on the summit of what is now known as the Rhoads Hill in Crown Point. From this lofty eminence they had a splendid view of the tract of land heretofore mentioned, a view of Lake Champlain for several miles in length, besides an extensive view into the state of Vermont, and to use their own words, " it was splendid to behold."— After feasting their eyesight on this beautiful landscape to their satisfaction, they left the mountain and camped that night on the bank of Putt's Creek, at the place now known as Buck Hollow. A few minutes with hook and line secured them a bountiful trout supper, and they then laid down to rest. The next morning bright and early found them out with hook and line again, and after a splendid breakfast of the speckled beauties they all wended their way to their respective homes in Vermont.

Well, time passed on till June, 1801, when my father in company with Abner Newton and Solomon Chase, returned to the wilds of Crown Point, built them a camp and worked together till each one had a fallow cut of some three acres, then returned to Vermont. The next September found them in Crown Point again ; they burned their fallows, and by the assistance of each other and some other new beginners, who, by this time, had commenced in like manner for themselves, in a few days each man had a comfortable log cabin ready for the reception of their families, and the next February my father moved his family, which consisted of his wife and three children, into his newly made home, myself being the youngest child, but two months old at the time. From this time the emigration from Vermont and New Hampshire received a new impulse, and in the space of two years some forty families from these states had settled on the wild lands in western Crown Point. At this period the lands were not surveyed or claimed by any one. In 1805, Wm. Cockburn and Goldsbrow Bangor put in an appearance from Kingston, Ulster County, N. Y. They claimed the lands, surveyed them, and sold them to the settlers at prices ranging from three to four dollars per acre. My father's lot proved to be Lot No. 47 in Cockburn's Pattent, now owned by Edwin Floyd.

I now come to my earliest remembrance, which was the surveying of those lands. It may not be amiss at this period to mention the names of some of the first settlers, viz: Israel Douglass, Stephen Spaulding, Abner Newton, Solomon Chase, John Eastman, John Sisson, Joseph Lockwood, Ephraim Towner, Daniel Bascom, Elisha Rhoads, Levi Rhoads, Wm. Barrows, Josiah Converse, Simon Hart, Abijah Nichols, Asa Nichols, Elder Lamson, Amos Lamson, Enos Lamson, Joseph Searles, John Chillis, Thomas Scott and others.

For several years Elisha Rhoads kept a small store, made large quantities of potash, bought all the ashes he could of the new settlets, which was carefully saved by them while clearing their land; this little item of trade was of essential benefit to the youthful settlement. About this time a school was started and kept by Mrs.

Rhoads, in the same log room where they kept house and store also. Five little scholars, myself among the number, all seated on a pine slab bench with round poles for legs, comprised the school and its fixtures, and that was the place where I first learned my A B C.

In the earliest days of the settlement an old hunter by the name of Comfort Towner, whose name is still fresh in the memory of the oldest inhabitants of the town, made his home at my father's for a year or more, and hunted for a living. I have heard him say that he killed some forty deer the first year, all within one mile of our house. I have often heard the report of the old man's long gun near our clearing, and soon after see the old man emerge from the woods drawing a stately deer behind him up to our door. Occasionally when the inhabitants felt disposed to have a little luxury they would indulge in a trout fishing. My brother Miles, who was some five years my senior, would go with the neighboring boys and take me with them. We would go about a mile from our place in a southwest direction by the aid of marked trees, to the high falls on Putt's Creek, now known as Penfield's Grist Mill, and fish down stream as far as Rhoades' the distance of about one mile and would generally capture about thirty pounds of the speckled beauties, weighing from $\frac{1}{4}$ to $1\frac{1}{2}$ lbs. each.

In 1806, the inhabitants were called on to do military duty. The towns of Schroon, Moriah, Ticonderoga and Crown Point were warned to appear armed and equipped on the spot where Ilelan Buck now resides. Some 75 or 80 men comprised the whole army. I saw them march around among the smoking log heaps; for the land at that time was in the process of being cleared.— I remember well when the sheriff brought a ballot box and some votes to my father and told him that he was appointed, with Samuel Foot and Alexander McKenzie, to travel the regions of Crown Point all over, and collect every legal vote that could be found in town, and to meet at McKenzie's on a set day and count them, etc. This was accordingly done, and 44 votes was all that could be obtained. Since that time I believe there has been some place appointed to do the voting.

I well remember of riding with my parents in a wagon from the top of Army Hill to the lake, when there was but one house from that place to the widow Wilcox's —now Hammond's Corners—and not one from there to the lake, all woods; for about half the distance is a heavy pine forest, and as we neared the lake the timber dwindled down to scrub oak bushes and small pines, and we could not see the lake until we were within 30 rods of it, and at the time of which I speak Lake Champlain was about as desolate as the country around it. Some half a dozen sloops, perhaps as many more schooners comprised the entire craft of commerce on the lake, and not a wharf or warehouse to grace its shores from Essex to Whitehall, and none of any importance when there. Steamboats and canals had never been thought of at this time. It took from four to twelve weeks then to get any communication across the Atlantic. A man can travel now to any part of the globe in the same number of hours that he could of days forty years ago. Perhaps the young reader may think we had no recreation in the olden time, if so he is much mistaken, for we had our share and just as good, and much cheaper then than now. I will cite one case : In 1807, Elisha Rhodes built a hotel and dancing hall; the building still stands as a monument of early days and enterprise, and is known as the old Rookery at Buck Hollow. The building was finished in time for a New Year's ball, and the party assembled, and as horses were almost unknown at that time in the place, ox teams were brought into requisition, and which conveyed the blooming lads and lasses to and from the dance. One pair of oxen worth $75 or $80, would take along six or eight couple with ease, and a dollar or two pay the bill, whereas it now takes a $500 horse and a $500 carriage to convey a single couple, any distance ever so short, and perhaps they don't weigh to exceed one hundred pounds each, and from $10 to $25 to pay their bill.

CHAPTER II.

The names of the first settlers in the east and central part of the town—The first mills, 2d, etc.—The methods and means of the inhabitants to procure an honest living—The Algereens—The trip to Whitehall—The cold season of 1816, the famine of 1817, and the suffering of the inhabitants —A bountiful harvest, the clouds of gloom and sorrow pass away.

Names of the first inhabitants in the east and central part of the town—Robert Walker, Aaron Townsend, George and Alexander Trimble, the Barnetts, Murdocks, the Brooks, James Morrow, Sam'l Foot, Dennis Megar, Andrew Hardy, the Heustices, Crossmans, Bigelows, Drakes, Davises, Rogers, Hildreths, Newells, Stantons, Strongs, Kings, John Ranne, Elijah Grosvenor, and others, and Rodolphus Field the first Physician.

James Morrow built the first mills, kept the first Inn and store at Crown Point Centre, about the year 1800. In 1810, Allen Penfield, an enterprising young man of some means, from Pittsford, Vt., built a grist and saw mill, at what is now known as Irondale, to which property he made large additions, and retained it within his name, till the day of his death, aged 87 years. In 1811, Ebenezer Hopkins erected a grist and saw mill one mile farther down the stream at what is now known as Buck Hollow. These mills, although of the cheapest construction, were of the greatest importance to the youthful settlement.

From this period nothing of importance occurred to marr the peace and quietude of the people, till the war of 1812. During that war reports were frequently circulated that the enemy were on their way from Canada through the vast wilderness that lies between this settlement and the Canada line, for the purpose of getting possession of the old fort on Lake Champlain. These reports were believed by many, and caused a great many sleepless nights among the timid portion of the inhabitants, and that was all it amounted to.

I will now pass along to September, 1814, when we had an alarm that the nation felt. About 9 o'clock P. M. the alarm reached town; horses and men were running all night long, from house to house, and every person that could bear arms was warned to appear the next morning by the rising of the sun at the principal places in their respective towns throughout the country. The call was promptly obeyed, for sun rise found every man at his post. This was truly an exciting time; here could be seen people of all ages and conditions, from the old frosty head of eighty winters or more, down to the infant in its mothers arms. Here were men and women of all ages, assembled together, all one common family and one common cause. Here was borrowing and lending guns, hats, coats, boots and money, anything to help the cause or facilitate the march. One old man by the name of McAully, a cripple from birth, lent his hat and coat and offered to lend his crutches. About 10 o'clock the start was made for Plattsburgh, and all sworn to fight for their country's cause. There was a few days at home of suspense and uncertainty. All kinds of stories were in circulation in regard to the enemy's advance, but the most reliable information was favorable to our cause. The battle was fought on Sunday the 11th of September, but the result of the battle we did not know till the Tuesday following. Still near enough to hear the report of their guns, booming along our shores and vibrating against our mountains: the next Tuesday with a fair wind Captain Archibald Smith, of Whitehall, sailed up the lake with his sloop and scattered the welcome news along the eager shores of old Champlain.

This news spread like wild-fire back into the country around, and for a few days labor was partially suspended, and the time spent in the exchange of congratulations and hilarity.

From that time the people had no more fears from the wars, and they returned to the peaceable pursuits of life. I will here say to the generation of the present day you little know of the hardships, trials and sufferings that the pioneers undergo in settling a new country, in preparing the ground, so that the next generation can harvest the crop. At the time of which I am writing, there was not one half land enough cleared in town for the support of the inhabitants in it, and of course the deficiency must be made up some other way. You would of course ask the question, "How did the people live?" No branch of enterprise in town whereby they could earn the honest dollar any better way than to go into the old primeval forest, cut down the massive trees, burn them into ashes and then manufacture them into potash, then carry the potash to Vermont and sell it to some speculator who would always buy at some price. At the best this was a hard way to earn a dollar, but some took this method, while others in the winter season made shingles, staves, brooms, baskets, hay rakes, and all other wooden wares were manufactured and marketed in Vermont. Large quantities of maple sugar were annually made, and tons on tons of it has been transported on men's backs from Crown Point to Vermont, and either sold or exchanged it for something that they stood in need of, and when the season of haying commenced the early settlers in Crown Point would turn out, almost to a man, and go and help Vermonters cut their grass and grain. All this trade and traffic between the two states was no doubt a benefit to both parties at this date.

Vermont was several years in advance of New York in the improvements on their farms, and some of the leading ones felt their importance considerably and gave their wild neighbors the appellation of Algereens, so that it became a common saying among themselves as their harvest drew near, that plenty of Algereens would be along from York State by the time their services were needed. But it so happened of late that several of the young Algereens had stepped across the state line and bought up many of their best possessions, and told the old occupants to go their way in peace and sin no more.

In 1813, when the United States troops were stationed in Whitehall, but as often called Skeenesborough at that time, a speculation was discovered and set in motion by such of the inhabitants as had by this time got a little ahead in the world and of some of their neighbors, the plan was to charter a scow, load it with the surplus products, take it to Whitehall and sell it to the soldiers.— Accordingly a scow was hired of Sam'l Ranne, the ferryman. The produce was hauled to the lake, and put on board the craft; the cargo belonged to some ten or twelve

different men, and consisted of potatoes, onions and all
kinds of garden sauce ; down to squashes, mellons, and
cucumbers ; not forgetting the butter, cheese, and honey :
as each man chose to be his own super-cargo : this furnished the vessel with plenty of back-woods sailors, and
as none of them had ever been drowned, they did not
fear the water ; by the aid of a few bed blankets and a
good north breeze, they set sail for Whitehall, about the
first of October, and as none of them had ever been farther south than old Ti, they occasionally had to enquire
the way ; they had no other difficulty in finding the place
of their destination, which they reached the next day.
Late in the afternoon, they sold their cargo, to good
advantage to the troops, and purchased such articles as
desired. And after strolling about the City, for a day
or so to see its wonders, the Elephant and soforth, they
returned, I believe the same route, by which they went,
and after about a weeks absence reached home in safety ;
where they could sit by their own fire-sides, and tell their
families and neighbors, of the wonders, which they saw,
in Whitehall. One of the party by the name of Seaver,
who always admired a good horse, said " he had no idea,
that they had such fine horses in the Southern States,
until he went there and saw them himself." From this
time till 1816 the inhabitants followed their usual voca-
tion of improving their lands &c., until they were called
to experience the greatest calamity that can befall a nation. The cold summer of 1816 will be fresh in the
minds of all who lived at that time, and were old enough
to remember it. It extended all over the United States,
and Europe ; the sun did not seem to posess any more
heat than it does in November, and the weather was cold
and chilly, ice was formed in every month in the year in
some localities ; flurries of snow were frequent. I re-

member the 8th day of that June, the snow fell more
than half an inch deep, and the fields were white as far
as the eye could see, but it soon disappeared, the weather was cold and dry, yet a little corn and potatoes
were raised, in some favorable localities, but not one
fourth of the amount required for the use of the inhabitants, saying nothing about the dumb beasts, and something must be saved for seed another season, at length
the dreaded time arrived, the summer of 1817, when
starvation stared them full in the face ; the poeple did
the best they could, what could they do more. Some
families who were quite well to do in the world, lived
without bread many days, and for the poorer classes it
was still harder ; there were a few cases, and very few,
where some fortunate man had a little surplus of old
grain on hand, it was spared and divided among the people as long as it lasted, but at exorbitant prices; it made
but little difference whether a man had money or not,
the bread was not in the land ; I have seen the silent
tears roll down the face of the child, the parent, and
the grandparent, all under the same roof, because they
had no bread; these were times that tried the human soul.
The question arises, how did the people live? Well they
had cows, the streams were full of fish, and the woods,
with game, the fields and mountains furnished an abun-
dance of berries in their season, and in some cases when
one meal was finished a family council was held, to
devise something for the next; this being done, each one
would start off hoping to find their share of it. I have
been mentioning some extreme cases, but this was not
the situation of the people in general, but one thing is
certain there was not much boasting about it; the ripening
fields were daily watched, and as soon as it could be
done, the ripest heads were picked and carefully shelled

and cleaned by hand, and cooked into some kind of
pudding which satisfyed the gnawing hunger and made a
good substitute for bread, a bountiful harvest was gath-
ered, every one had bread and to spare, and the clouds
of gloom, which had so long enshrouded the land, gradu-
ally arose and passed away, like the sullen clouds after
the departed storm. A few days since while collecting
some statistics for this history, I called on Mr. John
Ober, a venerable old man of 82 summers, a man of
truth and veracity, who told me some of his hardships
and sufferings, during this trying season. He then had
a young family and was on a new farm; I will give you
his story as near as I can, in his own words; he said, "I
got completely up a stump, I heard that Col. Howe of
Shoreham, had some flour to sell, I took 96 lbs., of
potash in a bag, and my father took 45 lbs., in another,
and we started for Shoreham 12 miles distant, about sun
rise, and when we had got within about three miles of
Col's., my father gave out, and I took his load in addition to my own, and carried it the rest of the way, we
sold our potash, bought our flour and started for home
again; I had the flour of two bushels of wheat, and ten
pounds of coarse flour of my own, and father had what
flour his potash came to, and we had not got more than
half-way home, before my father gave out again, then I
took his load in addition to my own and carried it home
arriving after midnight. I tell you, the next day we
were pretty tired and sore." It is pleasant to know that
Mr. Ober has a competence in his old age, and surround-
ed by a large family of kind children, to smooth his path
to the grave. His neighbors like to listen to his tales of
truth and sorrow, as they fall from the lips of one of the
early pioneers who settled the back wilderness of old
Crown Point. This case was only one of the many of a

similar nature, but the actors in the drama have mostly passed away, with only now and then one left to tell the sorrowful story. Peace be to their ashes.

CHAPTER III.

The Champlain Canal, and the new era of light that dawned on the valley of Lake Champlain—Col. Howe builds the great dam. Incidents relative thereto—The people begin to think the desolate and worthless regions of the Adriondacks, may yet be turned to some account. Building the first saw-mill among the Adriondacks, names of the proprietors, incidents relative to raising the first mill &c.,

In 1818, the Champlain Canal was commenced and finished so far in 1819 that water communication was open for canal boats, between the Hudson river and Lake Champlain. By this enterprise new business was opened to this entire region, the spirit of enterprise awoke and set the ball in motion. An intrinsic value was placed on the vast wilderness of the Adrondacks, as well as on the ores and minerals of which the country abounded, these long neglected regions, began to be explored by men of enterprise in search of sites for manufacturing Lumber, Iron, &c., In 1819 the first enterprise of the kind was commenced among us, Col. Job L. Howe from Shoreham, Vt, built the famous dam across Putts creek at what is now Wymans lower mills; he employed about fifty men the whole season and kept a small store from which he entirely paid his help. A good chopper received 62½ cents per day, and a man with an ox team, one dollar per day. Then we paid one dollar for three yards of cotton shirting the same for calicos, and all other things in proportion; we sometimes thought the Col. rather steep in his prices, as he only had to go to Middlebury for his goods, but I suppose it was about as well as he could do by us ; at any rate it was as well as we could do ; there was no striking in those days for higher wages or better times, the men were glad to find a chance to work on almost any terms. It was my fortune at that time to drive an ox team, for six weeks drawing logs and timber for that dam; the Col. subsequently built several other mills which were supplied by this dam, which were in opperation for several years to his advantage, and the commonwealth of Crown Point and vicinity. In 1821, the first Co., was formed for lumbering purposes among the Adirondack mountains. It consisted of the following getlemen, Deacon Allen Penfield, Dea. Phineas Wilcox, Dea. Ebenezar Hopkins, and John Pressy, who was very far from being a deacon.

They purchased a small site, and a quantity of pine timbered land, on Paradox tract, at the place now known as the old Dudly mill, on Paradox creek ; at that time I worked for deacon Wilcox, and went with the rest of the company about a dozen in all some four miles into the wilderness, to make a beginning. A sight was selected and all went to work in earnest, to clear a spot for the house and mill, we had worked about five minutes when our title was disputed by a party numbering about a hundred to one of us, we all beat a hasty retreat, but soon returned equiped with fire brands, and torches, and soon vanished the foe, which proved to be nothing more nor less than a nest of black hornets; this is very fresh in my memory for I got my full share of the sensation produced at the time. A spot was soon cleared and a house erected, we then proceeded to fall and hew timber for the mill, which in four weeks was ready for raising, a general invitation was given to the inhabitants in town, and very generally accepted. They were elated with the thoughts of having something like business going on in their midst, where they could find employment near home at a specified time. About forty men turned out to raise that portion of the mill which was not finished the first day, consequently they must stay over night ; well there was enough to eat and drink; the reader must understand this occurred in days of yore, when bread was considered to be the staff of life, and whiskey, life itself ; when good fellows were plenty, but good templars rather scarce. The proprietors had furnished two large three gallon jugs of whiskey for the raising; it was understood that one was to be spared for the second day, the other was finished at a late hour the first night. The evening passed away pleasantly, each in turn telling stories, and singing such songs as were suitable on such an occasion, all then turned in for rest. The next morning found all on our feet, ready for a little whiskey, but to our astonishment the jug was gone, whiskey and all; some one had stolen and carried it away; here was a great dilemma and long faces by the dozen, everything as silent as the tomb, except the birds in the trees, which seemed to raise their notes higher than ever, and rejoice at our calamity; I suppose it was because they had no use for whiskey. Still no one knew anything about the lost jug, but from some unmistakable signs suspicion rested on one of our number by the name of Parker, an old soldier ; who was told very promptly to produce the jug, or take the beach wythe, so he provided himself with a forked stick or mineral rod used in searching for minerals, and after lining and cross lining for some time the spot was centered and the jug found, here we were every man, deacons and all, following the old soldier around searching in every nook for the lost treasure. There was another change, the whole company vociferously shouting which was answered by the owls, every face as bright as the rising sun ; now for the sake of a little variety, I will turn the crank of my poetry machine, once or twice to see if we can produce a rhyme in honor of this occasion, and here it comes

The Heavens wept, the earth rejoiced
    And Hell was very friskey,
That after two hours faithful search,
    We found the jug of whiskey.

Well, to shorten my story the mill was raised, and the whiskey drank, and after partaking of a sumptuous dinner of pork and beans provided by the noble firm, all left for their respective homes in high spirits thinking we did honor to ourselves and justice to the firm.

CHAPTER IV.

Howe's mill soon changed owners and passed into the hands of Hammond's Co.,—Their prosperity and the advantage it was to the inhabitants.—About this time Buck & Bailey came into town sold goods, manufactured lumber, &c.,—Several other mills were built by different parties.—Penfield & Taft, manufactured lumber for southern market.

Howe's mill soon changed owners, and passed into the hands of Hammonds & Co., who laid the foundation for their extensive lumbering enterprise, which they prosecuted with the utmost zeal and perseverance for about 40 years ; they also built several other mills and bought large additions to their former purchases, until they could travel some ten miles in different directions on their own lands ; which proved to be a source of great wealth to them ; as their profits were only known to themselves it is sufficient to say they made their pile honestly and at the same time it gave employment to every man in town who was disposed to work ; especially in the winter season ; and has been one of the principal main-springs to the prosperity of Crown Point.

About this time Buck & Bailey came in town, opened a store, and began lumbering operations ; they bought large tracts of pine timber, built mills, and for 10 years manufactured large quantities of lumber for the southern market. When the company dissolved partnership their property came into the hands of Hiram & Helan Buck, who subsequently sold their lumbering interest and gave their attention to agriculture, land speulations, &c.

During the next five years several other parties built mills and manufactured lumber on a smaller scale, viz.: Allen Breed, Ephraim Towner, M. & S. Spaulding ; Spear & Ensist, Wright & Pond, Wm. & H. Phelps, Johnathan Breed, Rhoads, Stratten, Brown, &c.,

All of these operations, although small when compared with larger ones, gave employment to a number of men ; and of course has been some advantage to the town. Penfield & Taft operated at Irondale, and manufactured large quantities of lumber for the southern market, getting their logs from the Adirondack mountains for several years. In 1834, Taft sold his interest to Penfield, since then the firm has been known as Penfield & Harwood, of whom I will say more hereafter.

Irondale Iron works are situated six miles west of the Lake, upon Putnam's Creek, which affords the motive power. The forge now contains four fires, one wooden helve hammer, weighing one thousand eight hundred pounds, and two wheels which were erected in 1828. It was until recently owned by Penfield & Harwood, who have sold their entire interest to J. & T.

Hammond, of Crown Point. The forge consumes charcoal, which is principally burnt in covered kilns about four miles from the works in the west part of Ticonderoga. Ore from the bed of the company, located about five miles from the works, among the Adirondacks, is used in the forge. It manufactures blooms and bars; the iron made in this forge has established the highest reputation. This statement is sustained by the fact that in 1829 the company received an order from the government for a large quantity of their iron to be fabricated into chain cables for the navy; it is extensively used for the fabrication of fine ware, and at Pittsburg it is used for making cast steel; the company have a separator near their works in which the ore is prepared for the forge; it is stated that two tons of separated ore yields a ton of Iron; the annual amount manufactured at this forge, is about five hundred tons, there are a saw mill and grist mill standing a few rods below the iron works and owned by the proprietors. Other minor industrial pursuits of Crown Point, embraced at the centre village three miles from the lake, viz. a tannery, woolen factory, grist mill and saw mill, tub and barrel factory, and wheel wright shop; one mile below are a sash and door factory and a pail and tub factory; still nearer the Lake are a grist and saw mill and wheel wright shop, all these works stand upon Putnam's creek, a small stream already mentioned.

Crown Point Iron Company's furnace: This work is situated ten miles west of Crown Point landing and was owned by that company consisting of J. & T. Hammond & E. S. Bogue, until recently E. S. Bogue sold his interest to J. & T. Hammond. A furnace was built on that site in 1845, burnt down in 1865, and immediately rebuilt. The stack is 42 feet high and nine feet across the boshes. It was a charcoal blast furnace ; the escape heat being used for generating steam for running blast, stamping ore, sawing coal brands and grinding feed ; 6,500 tons of ore and 650,000 bushels of charcoal were used annually, producing 3,500 tons of pig iron. During the last eight years the furnace was in operation only about three fourths of the time, owing to the insufficient supply of coal, which was burnt in kilns. The ore was taken from a bed owned by the company, one mile distant from the works, and the lime from a quarry about the same distance. This furnace has been peculiarly successful in its manner of operation and the quality of iron produced. Since the establishment of the Bessamer steel works at Troy, a large portion of the iron from this furnace has been purchased by that institution. The harder and higher qualities secure a constant market from the manufactories of malable iron. In consequence of it being made from charcoal, which became so scarce, this furnace was allowed to run down some three years ago, and has been burnt down since. The old stack still stands a monument of early enterprise, healthfully ensconced among some half dozen high barren peaks of the Adirondack mountains.

CHAPTER V.

Vermont loses her Algereens, becomes very friendly to us.—A short trip on Lake Champlain.

The early inhabitants of Crown Point were chiefly emigrants from Vermont and Newhampshire ; who brought their habits of industry, religion and politics with them. They have mostly passed away, only now and then one left to tell the story. Their offsprings are now the principal inhabitants of the town, and many of them business men and not entirely ignorant of a pioneers life in a new country. They have inherited the habits of industry and frugality, and generally have a competence, and are above want.

About the year 1821 they turned their attention to agricultural pursuits, more than ever, and found themselves well rewarded. In the winter season they hauled lumber, iron and iron ore to the lake, earning a hundred or two dollars, so that after defraying contingent expenses had something left for pin money : and here is where Vermont lost her Algereens. Still we respect our Vermont neighbors, because they frequently came and helped us haul our lumber, iron and iron ores to the Lake. I greatly respect old Vermont, for I was born there, and as Stephen A. Douglas once said, "it was a noble state to be born in, providing he emigrated very young."

Now if the reader will accompany me, we will take a little sail on old Lake Champlain. We will first take a look at the old garrison on long point, whose old grey walls stand as monuments of wars one hundred and thirty years ago ; when France and England, two mighty nations beyond the wide Atlantic were strugling with each other for their respective claims for possessions in this North American wilderness, the history of which is too well known for me to make many comments. After leaving the old Fort we will move along up the Lake, and observe the scenery along the western shore. There stands a beautiful light house, erected by the government, to aid the mariners who may navigate these waters in the night ; and further along behold those splendid farms and beautiful residences of the Murdocks, Trimbles, Barnets, Hunters, and Breeds ; all early settlers of this

town. Now we come to Wolcott's ferry, and the mouth
of old Putts creek, which after leaving its source, and
turning 101 water wheels it silently lands its wearied
waters in the bosom of the Lake ; half a mile further
on we arrive at Gunnisons wharf, ware house, steamboat
landing and ferry ; the ware house is filled with barrels,
boxes, crates, &c., all destined to their several owners
back in the country around. Now walk up this little
bank, and look there. Oh ! what a change—I stood on
this identical spot 68 years ago ; not a building could be
seen west of here, nothing but a forest, I now behold a
broad, handsome street, with a row of splendid white
buildings on either side, and among the rest, the first
house that was ever painted in this town. It was built
in 1814, by Wm. Livingston, Esq, and now occupied by
Wm. Scott. Now step with me into Gunison's spacious
and splendid Hotel, and take a glass of Saratoga water
with the good old deacon, and then move along to Hammonds wharf, and what do we behold ; massive piles of
iron, iron ore, lumber, brick and stone, and more than a
hundred laborers at work putting those materials together ; we also see a canal extending some 40 rods inland,
with a steam boat and several canal boats in it, on en-
quiry, we are told that Crown Point Iron Company are
building two extensive furnaces here and they are also
building a rail-road from this place 13 miles west to their
mines back among the Adirondack mountains where un-
told millions of wealth still lie hidden in the bosom of
the earth; of this I will say more hereafter. We will now
go to the lofty summit of the Rhoad's hill, and stand on
the spot where the old pioneers stood seventythree years
ago, and view the scenery before us; oh, what a splendid
panorama lies at our feet, the ten miles square of wilderness mentioned in the commencement of this history has

been turned into fruitful fields or farms well cultivated,
with orchards, yards and gardens, and on almost every
farm we can behold a large white dwelling which indica‑
ted the place where comfort dwells; they are now enjoy‑
ing all the blessings of civilization, peace and plenty ;
here we have extensive views of Vermont scenery, her
old green mountains as green as ever, arable land has
been generally well cultivated, and the inhabitants are
wealthy and respectable, and can boast of its being a
land of steady habits. Now as we shorten the angle of
vision and look at old Champlain once more where in
the early days of this history, you would scarcely see a
craft in motion, now the beautiful Lake is dotted all over
with commercial crafts of almost every description, mov‑
ing to and fro; the commerce of Lake Champlain now
large is every year augmented. The lumber the ore the
Iron, fabrics of the north, combined with the grain and
flour of the west, the coal and merchandise from the
South constitute a vast trade ; to their domestic resources
may be added the productions of Canada, which seek a
market by this avenue, and the goods chiefly bonded that
pass into the dominion from American ports, and much
of which is returned under fresh entries all swelling this
immense internal commerce. Numerous Canadian ves‑
sels designed for the navigation of the St. Lawrence are
really distinguishable from American by their peculiar
structure and appearance, reach the waters of Cham‑
plain via Chamblee canal; vessels from the upper Lakes
are frequently observed in our harbors. A large class
of the population contiguous to the Lake are connected
with its navigation.

CHAPTER VI.

Churches, stores, manufactories, &c.—Ores, when and by whom discovered.
The first Iron manufactured in Crown Point and by whom.

There are four churches in town, three of which are well attended, the fourth is an old affair and only occupied occasionally; six dry-goods and grocery stores, one druggist store, one hardware, two of stoves, tin, and sheet iron, one Tannery, one sash, door, blind, tub, and pail factory, three flouring mills, five saw-mills, three harness makers, two furniture stores, four hotels, and a goodly number of blacksmiths and shoemakers shops, and two physicians; which speaks well for the health of the place. The old iron companies ore bed was first discovered by Timothy P. Hunter in 1821, while hunting for bees; he brought some small specimens from the bed in his pocket, which he exhibited to his friends who kept it secret for about two years, at length it leaked out, and the location was generally known; it never benefited Mr. Hunter, he lived and died a poor man. Miles Spaulding and Otis Bradford were the first men that opened said bed, and took therefrom some 8 or 10 hundred pounds of ore, which they carried in bags on their backs through the wilderness over one mile to a road where a team could be had, which hauled it to Ticonderoga where it was tested, and pronounced genuine, but through the treachery of some of their confidential friends, this their chance for a fortune was lost, and also their labor.

The Penfield bed so called, but now owned by the Crown Point company, and was discovered in 1826, by a boy named Reuel L. Cram while hunting for partidge, taking hold a small bush to help himself up the mountain steep, the bush became detached from the rock and there lay the shining ore; he carried some specimens of it to his father, who was fortunate enough to own the land, and opened the bed ; he subsequently sold it to Penfield & Taft. Reuel Cram now resides in Pembroke, N.H. The Sax and Floyd bed was discovered by Samuel Renne in 1818 and opened by him 1822, quantities of it were taken to Plattsburg and manufactured into hollow ware; it has been mixed with other ores and worked to good advantage but of late has been allowed to rest; the iron business of Crown Point is destined to become a source of national wealth,it was initiated by John Ranne Esq., in 1823, in a small forge near Crown Point centre on the exact site where Shearer's wheel-wright shop now stands ; he obtained most of his ore from Cheever mine and occassionaly used some of the Sax and Floyd ore but used the Penfield ore after its discovery.

<hr />

CHAPTER VII-

The Whitehall and Plattsburg Railroad.—The people of Northern N. Y. ela- ted with the Governor's promise.—The town was bonded for $50,000 in aid of the Rail Road.—Contributions, and by whom. Rail Road built from Port Henry to Ticonderoga.—The Whitehall & Plattsburg Rail Road leased to Vermont Central. The Vermont Central sells the lease to the N. Y. & Canada R. R. Co.

The Whitehall and Plattsburg Railroad was surveyed in 1861 and work was commenced Feb. 20th, 1869, on the banks of Putts Creek. A petition was presented to the Legislature asking for $500,000 to aid in the construc- tion of the said road, $250,000 were granted; Gov. Fen- ton signed the bill, promising to sign another bill the next year if he was re-elected, and it passed both houses of the Legislature; this promise elated the people of northern New York, who had always been shut out from the outside world during the winter months. He was consequently re-elected by the vote of thousands of his political enemies. Another bill passed the Legislature to give another $250,000 to aid the construction of said road, but was vetoed by the Gevernor. But we do not think it worth while to waste time and paper in writing his eulogy,we only say he is like the dutchman's coon dog —good to tree the coon and bark at his master;the town was then bonded to the amount of $50,000 to aid in building the road, but was strongly opposed by many of our best citizens, who feeling the burdens of the late war, and other drafts on their resources, were unwilling to comply with the measure, but a majority ruled, and was done subsequently. Yankee enterprise took the case in hand, and raised a large amount by subscription which put the road in running order from Port Henry to Ticonderoga ; cars were running in less than two years, from the time work was commenced on it. This short road, only some sixteen miles in length, already pays $12,000 of our taxes; it is believed by many of our best men that the town bonds will prove a good investment for the town, and when the furnaces and Rail Road now in course of construction are completed, together with the mines, when worked, will pay one half of our taxes, besides giving employment to hundreds of laboring men, the entire year. The following named gentlemen contribu- ted the sums opposite their respective names.

Charles F. Hammond & Sons, $12,500.
E. S. Bogue,   3,000.
Penfield & Harwood,   2,000.
C. P. Fobes & Co.,   1,000.
J. C. Brevort,   500.
C. P. Iron Co,   1,000.
                              _____
                               $20,000

State aid being refused, and the counties south of us feeling little interest in the Whitehall and Plattsburg R. R, probably because they had a railroad of their own, and that was enough, consequently the Whitehall and Plattsburg R. R. was leased to the Vermont Central in 1871. They bridged the Lake at Ticonderoga and built a branch R. R., from the Lake to Licester Junction. Opening a communication between Port Henry and Boston, and also to New York, by a roundabout way through Vermont. The New York and Canada R. R. was surveyed in 1871 and work was commenced. On account of its close proximity to the Whitehall & Plattsburg R. R., from Ticonderoga to Port Henry, the N. Y. & Canada R. R., bought the lease and consolidated by a special act of the N. Y. Legislature in 1873.

Charles F. Hammond sold his interest to J. & T. Hammond in 1866. E. S. Bogue, Penfield & Harwood sold their respective interests to J. & T. Hammond in 1872. The present Crown Point Iron Company was formed, in Oct., 1872, with a cash capital of $1200,000.

CHAPTER VIII.

A view of the mines and surrounding scenery.—A fancy Rail Road ride from the mines to the Lake.—The improvements and prospects of the town. —Universal improvements.—The effects of science, and the conclusion.

Dear reader, a person is well paid in taking a trip to the Adirondacks, and stand at the mines which is a splendid place to view the scenery for miles around; think of the past and take observations. Here are some three hundred men employed in raising Iron ore, one half of them perhaps, far down in the mines under our feet, and others at the mouths of the shafts. Powerful steam en-

gines are raising the ore from the mines as fast as it is
ready for its assent.   Here is also a beautiful young village, built expressly for the use of the miners; north and
west of us are the high and barren mountain peaks made
bare first by the woodman's ax, and then by subsequent
fires.   South of us, and in plain sight, there is another
party of miners at work on the northern declivity of a
sister mountain, raising iron ore for the Ticoderoga Co.;
numerous other beds have been opened in the vicinity,
which proves that the entire region around us an immense
deposit of mineral wealth; and on the east of us stands
old Nob mountain with lofty brow far above all the others.
It seems like a lonely sentinel guarding the immense
wealth which lies at its feet.   Here are massive piles of
rich ore recently torn from the bowels of the mountains, which soon must take its leave of its kindred ele-
ment, and be manufactured into various shapes and uses
for the benefit of civilization, in every part of the globe.
From this standpoint the rail road takes its start for the
Lake, and the new furnaces.   But as the new rail-road is
not quite completed we shall be obliged to take the fancy
train from here to the Lake, and here it comes—we are
now on board the cars, and under way, we shall stop a
minute or so at the principal stations on the way; how
still and easy these cars run, and the engine makes no
noise at all, here on our left are the ruins of an old furnace, which was built by the old Crown Point Iron Co.,
in 1845, and run by that company some 26 years or
more with good success, but as fuel became scarce was
allowed to run down, and since then has been consumed
by fire; its principal business was the manufacturing of
pig iron.   We are now passing through an uneven
country, with a few good farmers where the inhabitants
are both industrious and prospering.   Irondale, the Con-

ductor says ; this is a pleasant little village which is owned
by the present Crown Point Iron company, its principal
business manufacturing bloom iron. We are off again,
this old and dilapidated village on our left, is Buck Hollow; it was once the most business place in Crown
Point.. This fine establishment on our right is the resi-
dence of Helan Buck; that lofty eminence on our left and
about one mile away, is the old Rhoades Hill, where our
history began. We are now swinging around the north
side of the Army Hill, where we have a fine pros-
pect of the north part of the town, the Lake and Vermont. Bradford Corners, the Conductor says; this is a
beautiful situation, but the rail-road hurts the looks of it
very much, and takes some of his best land from him,
but he has enough left yet, to work himself to death on.
We are off again, passing through some good farms and
over some deep gulfs, but the road is perfectly smooth,
till we hear the Conductor say Hammonds Corners; this
is a nice little village with a fine brick church, a splendid
park, a soldier's monument, which was the gift of one
individual, to perpetuate the memory of the brave boys
who for their country fell. We have come to a perfect
stand-still, but we are on the temperance side of Vial's
Hotel.

I have endeavored to fulfill my promise to the reader
in showing him Crown Point as it was seventy three
years ago, and picture out to him some of the hardships
and sufferings of the inhabitants and early pioneers of
this town according to the best of my abilities. Also its
rise and progress from time to time as things transpired,
and some of the principle causes thereof.

And as there never was an effect without a cause, I
will endeavor to show him some of the principle causes
of its present appearance and future prospects at the

present day. As the past has been explained I will speak
of the present and the future; there are immense depos-
its of iron ore of the best quality known to exist, at the
mines among the Adirondacks, is the first cause. The
second is we have a few enterprising men among us who
are determined to develop their wealth and make them
useful to the world at large; for this purpose there are
two immense Furnaces now being built at the Lake, and
a rail road from the furnaces to the mines, a distance of
13 miles for the express purpose to convey the ores from
the mines to the furnaces, and to the Lake.

There is also a canal some forty rods long from the
Lake extending inland to the Furnaces, to facilitate the
mammoth enterprise. And the question comes up where
are the men, and who is the man, that keeps this mighty
wheel in motion and employs 800 laborers daily, who
are well paid for their services. The answer is, it is
through the indefatigable energy and enterprise of Gen.
John Hammond.

But let it be understood, that these blessings are not
all confined to Crown Point, alone, or to any particular
locality. Some of them are the productions of scienti-
fic men, in different parts of the globe, but mostly in
our own county. When I meditate on the great change
that has taken place since my remembrance, I become
lost in wonder, and turn my attention to some other sub-
ject. It seems as though man had almost aspired to be
a Deity; he has called the lightnings down from the
clouds, and caged them up in bottles, he has harnessed
them up, and made them do the office of our post boys.
He has called down the Sun beams and made them paint
our pictures for us, he has analized the air, he has meas-
ured the depth of the ocean, he has bound the earth in
iron bands and a girdle of electricity encircles the globe.

And what is done in one hemisphere is immediately known in another. And at this time they have crafts already made, to navigate mid air to other continents; and with the same ratio of progress for the next century as in the past, he will have the most essential powers of nature under his controll. My story is told, I was only about four years old when I introduced myself to the reader, and now at the age of seventy-two years I leave him and bid him a long and pleasant good bye.

SAMUEL S. SPAULDING.

Crown Point, N. Y., Sept. 24th., 1873

The Assessors Roll of Crown Point in 1818, was as follows.

Real Estate,	$81,155
Personal Property,	20,062
And the Tax was,	664,18

Names of the taxable Inhabitants at that date.

Armstrong, Jewit	Adams, Levi
Allen, Benjamin	Adkins, Seth
Adkins, George	Allen, David
Amy, Abraham	Amy, John
Austin, Rodman	Abbot, Obed
Bigalow, John	Bigalow, Amos
Bigalow, Eben	Bigalow, Levi
Butterfield, Stephen	Bishop, John F.
Burrows Wm. L.	Brooks, Jonathan
Brooks, Daniel	Bouge, Ethan
Bradford, Simon	Blackman, John
Bascom, Daniel	Breed, Allen
Barnett, James H.	Balou, George

Barrit, Nathan

Boyington, Joel

Barnett, Asa W.

Bennet, Lewis L.

Burdet, Israel

Chilcott, Amos

Coburn, Charles

Chapin, Aaron

Chapin, Justice

Nichols, Asa

Nichols, Zadock

Nichols, Amasa

Nichols, Aaron Cedar

Nims, Rufus

Ober, Israel

Ober, Benjamin

Perkins, Wm.

Phillips, Amaziah

Phipin, Clark

Rhoads, Levi

Reed, George

Rogers, Daniel

Rogers, John

Simond, P. Nathan

Stowel, Royal

Shattuck, Samuel

Stratten, Benjamin

Seaver, Perly

Sisson, John J.

Chapman, Calvin

Chellis, Abraham

Converse, Elijah

Cutter, Jonas

Chapin, Edmond B.

Barrit, Reuben

Barrows, Samuel

Butterfield, Wilder

Burrows, Jesse

Chilcott, John

Chilcott, Abijah

Cummings, Thomas

Chapin, Justine

Cooper, Zebade

Nichols, Asa 2d

Nichols, Albe

Nichols, John

Nichols, Aaron, Sugar Hill,

Ober, Samuel

Ober, John

Pulcifer, Amos

Pickett, W. John

Phillips, Reuben

Rhoads, Elisha

Renne, John

Russel, Wm.

Russel, Nehemiah

Smith, Benjamin

Stowel, Asa

Stowel, David

Sprague, Nathan

Searl, Joseph

Sisson, John

Sawyer, Ephraim

Chellis, John

Converse, Josiah

Cole, Amos

Cram, Amos

Clark, Abraham

Crossman, John

Crossman, Ira

Dudey, James

Drake, David

Drake, Joseph

Davis, Elijah

Dibble, John

Davis, Hammond

Fuller, Joseph

Farnsaworth, Thomas

Farewell, Jesseniah

Foot, Samuel J.

Gedding, John

Griswoold, Jonas B.

Grosvenor, Elijah

Hews, Barney

Hildreth, Leonard

Hustice, Benjamin B.

Huestice, Timothy

Hildreth, James

King, John

Kellog, Sylvester

Lamson, Stephen

Livingstone, Wm.

Lyon, Jesse

Lamson, Horace

Magowan, Berny

Magennis, John

Murdock, Samuel

Nichols, Andrew

Newel, Wm.

Nelson, Wm.

Stratton, Jabes

Scoot, Isaac

Crossman, Elijah

Catlin, John B.

Drake, David

Drake, David

Dunlap, Horace

Davis, Daniel R.

Davis, Willard

Edmund, Stephen

Foster, Franklin M.

Fuller, Aron

Foot, Samuel

Field, Rodophus

Glidding, Thomas

Griswoold, Alexander

Hunter, Stephen

Hopkins, Ebenezer

Hildreth, Jeremiah

Hustice, Wm. B.

Holden, Joshua

Jenks, Jeremiah

Kemp, O. P.

Lewis, James

Lamson, Ezekiel

Lamson, Elder

Lane, Henry G.

Meritt, Joseph

Makenzie, Robert

Munroe, Royal

McAlly, Susan

Miles, Spaulding

Newel, Seth

Newel, Joshua

Scott, Thomas

Turner, Thomas

Taft, Timothy

Thompson, Amos

Trimble, A. Chilon

Willcox, Asa

Willcox, Phineas

Wilder, Daniel

Wilkins, Isaac

Wright, Peter

Lockwood, Joseph

Maynard, Abner

Smith, Reuben

Rowley, Henry

Bartlet, Moses

Morse, Benjamin

Town, Silas

Barker, Samuel

Lamson, Enos "estate"

Joshua, Holden

Towner, Ephraim

Tuttle, Harvey

Townsend, Aaron

Wood, Abel

Walker, James

Ward, Roswell

Wheeler, E. Aaron

Witherbee, Thomas

Maynard, Heman

Smith, James

Town, Joseph

Rowley, Hiram

McIntyre, Moses

Town, Ira

Quartemas, Martin

Reed, Benjamin

Smith, Samuel

Treadway, William

The Assessor's Roll of Crown Point in 1835, was as follows:

Valuation of Real Estate, $91,361

" Personal Property $4,800

The Tax was $750,22

Names of the taxable inhabitants at that date :

Adkins, George	Austin, James	Adams, Levi
Armstrong, Martin	Armstrong, Jewet	Aldin, Milo
Alden, William	Avrel, Samuel	Allen, Benjamin
Barnett, Jedediah	Benedict, Jonas	Ballou, Amos
Barnett, James	Breed, Allen	Ballou, Hiram
Baldwin, John	Burge, Nancy	Barker, Samuel
Burwell, John	Barret, Joseph	Barret, Reuben

Bixby, Jacob	Boyington, Joel	Barrows, Zoraster
Ballou, George	Bigalow, Eben	Brooks, John B.
Bishop, John F.	Breed, Jonathan I	Breed, Jared
Bradford, Otis	Bradford, Enos	Brooks & Floyd,
Barret, Lucian	Barnett, Asa W.	Barber, James
Bigelow, John	Buckman, Silas	Buck, Hiram
Bishop, Gerome	Breed, Allen	Brown, George
Brown, Forrest	Bartlet, Eumanas	Brooks, Daniel
Breed, Foster	Barker & Fenton,	Bradford, Orren
Brooks, Jonathan	Bailey, Abel	Barrows, Henry
Barrows, John	Baker, George	Bailey, Samuel B.
Clark, Stillman	Crossman, Ira	Cross, William
Chilcott, John	Call, Luther	Chilcott, Abijah
Coburn, Charles	Cory, Lewis	Cleaveland, Daniel
Cross, Warren	Converse, Josiah	Chapin, Aaron
Cram, Asa	Cummings, Leon.	Cutter, Charles
Conn, George jr.	Crossman, Aburn	Dunkley, Lucius
Davis, Calvin	Davis, Elisha	Drake, Stephen
Davis, Hammond	Davis, Orson	Davis, Benjamin S.
Davis, Bradley M.	Dibble, Thomas	Dudley, Ezra
Douglass, Jona.	Dean, Timothy	Derby, Lemuel
Drake, Lyman	Drake, Lyman	Davis, Henry
Drake, David	Dike, Franklin F.	Edmunds, Afred A.
Ewen, John T.	Foot, Samuel	Fisher, Leonard
Farr, Abijah	Farnsworth, Thos.	Fuller, Aaron
Foster, Moses	Floyd, John	Fenton, Chauncey
Giddings, John	Gracy, Robert	Goodrich, Elijah
Griswould, Alex'r	Gileo, Nichols	Glidden, Josiah
Glidden, Asahel	Gibson, Gabriel	Gunnison, George
Gray, Osro P.	Gracy, James	Groves, John
Hunter, Stephen	Hutchison, James	Hale, Henry
Hodgman, Thos.	Hildrith, Hollis	Hildrith, Thomas
Howe, Lemuel D.	Hughes, Bernard	Hammond, Cha's F.
Howe, Juba	Howe, Henry	Hammonds & Co.
Hascall, Libeas	Holden, Joshua	Heustice, Daniel
Heustice, Timothy	Heustice, Benj.	Heustice, Daniel D.
Hildrith, Norman	Hodgeman, Tim.	Ingalls, Samuel H.

Ingalls, Hibbard	Jencks, Jeremiah	Johnson, Timothy
Jackson, Elias	Knowls, Arthur	Knowlton, Thomas
Kibby, Arrial A.	Kendal, Caleb	King, John
King, John jr.	Lane, Robert	Lewis, Samuel
Mamson, Stephen	Lock, John M.	Livingston, Wm.
Leeland, Martin	Lawrence, Jedediah	Morton, Joel
Mason, Lorenzo	Morton, Lym'n & L.	Morton, Loyal
McAully, Susan	Mills, William	Maginis, Aaron
Maginis, John	Murdock, Samuel	Murdock, James
Murdock, Sam'l jr	Moore, John	Moore, Levi
Moore, William	Moore, John E.	McIntyre, Micager
McIntyre, Abijah	McAully, Smith	Monroe, Loyal
Morgan, Roswell H.	Mott, John R.	Nichols, Aaron
Nichols, Amasa	Nickerson, Amos	Nims, Rufus
Nilson, Aaron	Nilson, William	Nilson & Allen
Nichols, Zadock	Newell, Joshua	Newell, William
Nichols, Asa	Ober, John	Ober, Joseph
Pond, Benager	Perkins, William	Porter, William
Pulsifer, Amos	Parmerter, Jacob J.	Pressy, John
Philips, Harvey	Penfield & Taft,	Philips, Ameziah
Prible, Paris I.	Potter, Moses	Prible, Abraham
Petty, John	Petty, Solomon	Pratt, Charles
Rogers, John	Russell, Hubbard	Russell, Jonathan
Rhoades, Levi	Rhoades, Elisha	Reed, Randal
Reed, Harris	Reed, Foster	Renne, John
Russell, Samuel (Black-smith)	Russell, Samuel (Inn-keeper)	
Rogers, Daniel	Rogers, Ward	Smith, Phineas
Smith, Frederick	Sprague, Nathan	Spaulding, Miles
Spaulding, Samuel	Stiles, Samuel	Spaulding, Caleb
Stanard, Joel	Searls, Joseph	Searls, Ransom
Spaulding & Hatch,	Sawyer, Abel	Sisson, Hiram
Sisson, John	Sturtefant, Alex S.	Sawyer, Chan'y P.
Stratten, Amos	Spaulding, Ira	Spaulding, Stephen
Simmonds, Hiram	Spaulding, S'n 2d	Simons, N. T.
Smith, Austin	Shattuck, Weston	Strong, Colburn
Sprague, Hiram	Stanton, James	Stanton, Elisha
Stanton, Amos	Spear, Alden	Stowel, Royal

Stowel, David	Scofield, William	Towner, Shaler
Towner, Ephraim	Towner, Ephrim I.	Towner, Ichabod A.
Towner, Ira	Towner, Benj. F.	Thrasher, Henry
Town, Silas	Town, Job	Train, Jonathan
Trimble & Murdock,	Thompson, Oka	Thompson, George
Taylor, John	Trimble, Chilon A.	Trimble, George
Titus, William	Taylor, Daniel	Turner, Septamus
Townsend, Moses B.	Townsend, Aaron B.	Townsend, John
Tyrell & Chipman,	Tyrill, James	Wood, Abel
Wolcott, Ariel	Wood, Jotham	Wallace, John I.
Wheeler, Aaron	Woodworth, John	Wilkins, Isaac
Whitman, Benj.	Whitman, Chauncey	Wright, Samuel
Wolcott, Moses	Wright, Peter	Wallace, John
Wilder & Gray,	Wilder, Joseph T.	Wrightonton, Geo.
Witherbee, Thomas	Witherbee & Wood	Wright & Eaton,

The Assessor's Roll of Crown Point in 1872, was as follows:

Valuation of Real Estate		$436,716
" Personal "		$38,750
The Tax was		$12,643,83

Names of taxable Inhabitants at this date :

Averel, Charles	Averel, Samuel	Adkins, Owen H.
Allen, John	Allen, Solomon	Allen, Leander A.
Avery, Horatio	Abeare, Antoine	Abbott, Seth
Allen, William	Breed, Eleazer	Barnett, Hyde R.
Breed, William	Breed, Foster	Barnett, James K.
Bevins, Benj. L.	Breed, Benjamin	Barnett, George
Barnett, Edward J.	Broughton, Darwin	Burdict, John C.
Bigalow, Daniel	Barker, Samuel H	Bradford, Otis
Brown, George	Barker, Elmore	Barker & Wyman
Brevoort, Julius C	Bascom, D. W.	Baldwin, Philo
Bigalow, Augustus	Bradford, Enos	Bradford, Aldin

Brooks, Daniel	Brooks, Jon. H.	Bigelow, Charles
Buck, Hiram	Bogue, Edwin S.	Barrows, William
Bowman, Ann	Barrows, Daniel	Barnett, Mercia I.
Bradford, Stewart	Bennett, Sophia	Babcock, Sarah
Bryden, James	Bly, Norman	Bradford, Orren
Brooks, Erving	Brooks, Wm.	Barret, Alvin & Reu.
Breed, Jon. I.	Breed, Sarah Ann	Baldwin, Martin
Boyington, Charles	Burrows, John	Baldwin, Ezra H.
Bigalow, Levi	Brooks, John B.	Bell, Charles
Bigalow, Calvin	Barnett, Wm.	Bushnell, Fred'k N
Baldwin, John	Buckman, Ahira	Barnett, Joseph
Brown & Rhoades	Bailey, Hilah	Bartlett, Joseph
Baldwin, Wm.	Burgy, James	Barton, Augustus
Barton, Wm. A.	Bell, Philo H.	Barton, Wm. H.
Bunel, Alonzo M.	Bailey, Abel H.	Bascom, Chester
Buck, He. & Al.	Bradford, Wesley	Buck, Helon
Blossom, Eliza	Buck, Almeda (Exr)	Crossman, Wm. H.
Crossman, A. S.	Crossman, Samuel	Curut, Wm.
Capron, Welc. D.	Carlisle, Amasa	Carter, Jeremiah B.
Cheney, Hiram	Chapin, Justin	Carter, Leander
Chapman, Geo. E.	Coburn, Frederick	Clune, Wm.
Clough, Edwin	Crough, Lawrence	Curtis, Amos
Cook, Wm. H.	Casey, Thomas	Carr, Henry
Coburn, James A.	Craw, Asa L.	Cowin, Thomas
Clough, Philip	Crawford, James	Carrol, Dacy
Cowin, James	Cram, Wm.	Champine, Francis
Crown Point I. Co.	Dsvis, Martha M.	Davis, Truman E.
Davis, James	Davis, Ozias S.	Dudley, Erving
Dwinel, Nehemiah	Depoutee, A. G.	Dunckley, Charles
Dudley, James	Davis, Warren	Davis, Elisha
Davis, Joseph	Depoutee, Moses	Dudley, Chauncey
Dahar, Mitchell	Drake, Elijah	Dolph, Sarah
Depoutee, Dennis	Deshan, George	Dudley, Henry
DeWolf, Charles	Fenton, Chauncey	Fuller, William
Fobes, Cyrus P.	Fobes, C. P. & Co.	Floyd, William
French, Isaac	French, Stillman	Farr, Elizabeth
Friend, Farewell	Fish, Samuel	Fleming, Alexander

Floyd, Edwin, R.	Fitch, Hiram	Fitch, Albert
Fitch, Alonzo	Freeman, Joseph	Goodrich, Joseph
Gunnison, George	Gunnison, William	Goodale, Phebe
Gonyo, Peter	Gregory, George A.	Gay, Eugene
Gracy, Robert	Gillet, Mark	Glidden, Joseph
Gilco, Fernando	Gado, Eli	Graham, William
Garvey, Patrick	Gray, George	Heustice, John
Hunter, Theodore	Hutchison, Adeline	Heustice, Calvin W.
Heustice, Timothy	Howe, Juba	Holt, Eliza B.
Hammond, Thos.	Hammond, John	Hammond, J. & T.
Hammond, Chas.F.	Heustice, Alpheus	Hildrith, Hart'l H.
Hurlbert, Warner	Heustice, Horace	Harrington, Edson
Hamilton, John	Harington, Rinaldo	Hunsden, John
Hamilton, Henry	Hammond, Mich'l	Hamilton, Arthur
Hutchison, Wm.	Hogan, Patrick	Holden, Joseph
Hitt, Wm. G.	Hadley, Thomas	Hadley, Helon
Hunter, Mathew	Hunter, Alexr.	Honsinger, Alvin
Horicon Iron Co.	Harwood, Van Ess	Hitt, Elery
Hodskins, Milton	Ingleston, Chaun.	Ingleston, Wm.
Ingalls, Nathan	Ingalls, Harrison	James, Wm.
Jordon, Edward	Kingsland, David	King, John jr.
Knapp, Bradford	King, Jonas	King, Jonas G.
Knowles, Arthur	Knights, Sydney	Kelly, James
Kellogg, James	Kellogg, Ephraim	Knowlton, Alfred
Kent, Enoch	King, Albert	Leland, Walter A.
La France, Joseph	Lock, Sophia	Lock, Alonzo
Lamos, Moses, B.	Lindsey, Robert D.	Labombard, John
Lavanway, Ransom	La Mountain Elihu	Lock, Theodore
La Co, Edward	Lee, Benjamin	Lock, Thomas B.
Lane, John	Lavine, Joseph	Lock, John M. Jr.
Lock, John M	Little, John	Lawrence, James
Lang, John	Lyford, John W.	Murdock, Samuel
Murdock, Jas. A.	Murdock, F. S.	Murdock, S. A.
Murdock, Jos. B.	Murdock, Jas.	Monty, Andrew
McNeal, Isaac	McNeal, Chas.	Moore, Horace
McAully, Norman	Morse, Hull	McDonough, Frank
McDonough, And.	Moore, Alvaris	Moncreaf, Wm.

Sprague, Samuel	Stanton, Elisha	Spaulding, S. S.
Starling, Calvin	Stanton, Amariah	Spaulding, Nelson
Stanton, Uriah	Sprague, Orland	Spaulding, La F.
Sartwell, Leonard	Starling, Wm. H.	Stowel, Horace
Stratten, Mary J	Spaulding, Hi. D.	Stiles, Benj. L.
Sage, Benjamin L.	Stevens, Charles	Smith, David R.
Spaulding, Sam. S.	Spaulding, A. V.	Sisson, George
Smith, Caroline	Sartwell, Willham.	Shepherd, Warren
Towner, Warren	Trimble, George	Trimble, Charlott
Townsend, M. B.	Townsend, Aaron T.	Taylor, Matilda
Thompson, Rufus	Thompson, Hepsy	Thrasher, Wm.
Tucker, Amelia	Taylor, Robert M	Thrasher, O. F.
Thompson, Alex.	Towner, John	Town, Daniel J.
Trainer, James	Turner, Septimus	Taft, Henry
Towner, Ephraim J.	Town, Selas	Towner, Ephraim
Town, Seth	Thrasher, Jane	Town, Harris
Thompson, D. A.	Thompson, Geo. H.	Thompson, Amos D.
Taft, James	Turner, Hiram F.	Vial, Alanson
Voree, Lewis B.	Vilmore, Nelson	Waterman, Chas.
Wood, John H.	Waterman, Albert	Waterman, Robert
Waterman, A. & R.	Warner, Franklin	Washburn, Chas. M.
Wood, Ashley	Wood, Harvey	Winters, Horatio
Wyman, Nahum R	Wyman, Henry E.	Wyman, Wm. W.
Wright, Hiram	Wait, Otes	Ward, Elias
Whipple, Wm.	Warner, Samuel	Worcester, Francis
Webster, Jared	Wells, Almon	Wolcott, Ariel (est.)
Wood, Horatio	Wright, Susan	Wolcott, Mary. A.
Wolcott, Samuel	Wood, Hapilona	Wyman, Daniel
Wolcott, Judson	Wells Henry, D.	Winters, Samuel
Wood, Russell	Witherel, James	Wolcott, Roger A.
Whitehall & Plattsburgh R. R.		Ward, John
Wait. Frank		

The reader will perceive, by examining the three Assessment Roll's, that only three persons paid a tax each time, viz: John Ober. Amos Pulcifer, & Ephraim Towner.

Mr. Towner was assessed in 1872, but died before the tax was collected. Mr. John Ober is now (Nov. 20, 1873) the only survivor of the three.

www.ingramcontent.com/pod-product-compliance
Lightning Source LLC
Chambersburg PA
CBHW021444090426
42739CB00009B/1627